Going West: Cowboys and Pioneers

Special Edition
Created by Angel Entertainment Inc.

Published in the U.S. by
Marboro Books, a division of
Barnes and Noble Bookstores, Inc.

Library of Congress Cataloging-in-Publication Data

Courtault, Martine.

   Going west, cowboys & pioneers/written by Martine Courtault;
illustrated by Donald Grant; translated by Vicki Bogard.

   Translation of: Vers L'Ouest, cowboys et pionniers.

   Includes index.

Summary: Briefly describes the movement of pioneers westward
across the United States and the kinds of work that came about
as a result of this, such as cowboys, trappers, and prospectors.

1. Pioneers — West (U.S.) — History — Juvenile literature.
2. Frontier and pioneer life — West (U.S.) — Juvenile literature.
3. West (U.S.) — History — Juvenile literature. 4. Cowboys — West
(U.S.) — History — Juvenile literature. [1. Frontier and pioneer
life — West (U.S.) 2. West (U.S.) — History] I. Grant, Donald,
ill. II. Title. III. Title: Going west, cowboys and pioneers.
IV. Series: Young Discovery Library (Series); 21.   89-5365
F596.C8313   1989   978'.02   ISBN 0-944589-21-9

Printed and bound by L.E.G.O., Vicenza, Italy

Written by Martine Courtault
Illustrated by Donald Grant

Specialist Adviser:
*Michael Dillon, former
member, Bronx River Scouts*

ISBN 0-944589-21-9
First U.S. Publication 1989 by
Young Discovery Library
217 Main St. • Ossining, NY 10562

YOUNG DISCOVERY LIBRARY

Westward ho!

The date: May, 1830
The place: Independence,
Missouri. When the leader
gave the signal, whole families
started off in caravans of
sturdy, canvas-covered wagons
pulled by horses or oxen.
This is the beginning
of a new life.

The early wagons were Conestogas,
in use since colonial days. Later
a shorter type, called "prairie
schooners," were most popular.

They were pioneers, the first people to push westward into the frontier. Their journey could last five or six months, leading them through vast plains and over the Rocky Mountains. It was a hard and dangerous trip, but the pioneers hoped to find a better life in the west. Some would farm the land and grow corn or wheat.

Others would raise cattle.

Most important—**the land was free!**

eagle

moose

coyote

OREGON

wolverine

fox

wolf

chipmunk

badger

cougar
(puma)

CALIFORNIA

bison (American buffalo)

antelope

prairie dog

rattlesnake

N

W E

S

MEXIC

8

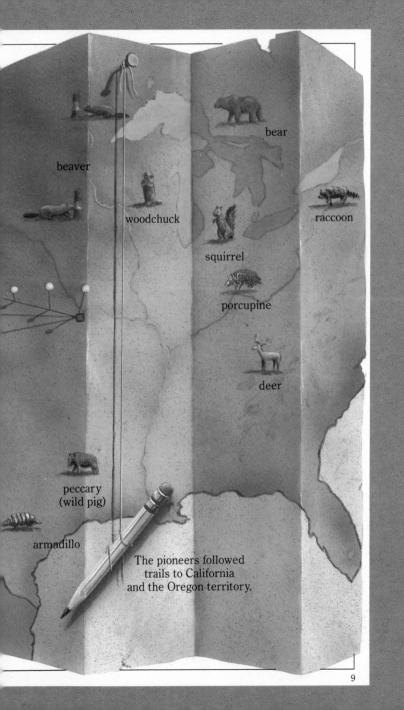

beaver

bear

woodchuck

raccoon

squirrel

porcupine

deer

peccary
(wild pig)

armadillo

The pioneers followed
trails to California
and the Oregon territory.

It took a long time to get ready.
The pioneers had to take many things
because there were no stores along
the trail. Barrels of food were piled
in the wagon: bacon and beans, dried
fruit. Cornmeal and sugar. Coffee and
tea. Pepper and ginger.

A large trunk held wool shirts and
trousers for the men, wool-and-linen
dresses for the women. The family sold
furniture or gave it away to friends, but
usually took the rocking chair along!
The butter churn and the candle molds
would come in handy. So would the ax,
saw, shovel and pick. A rifle was
needed for hunting.

The prairie stretched as far as the eye could see. Often there was not a single tree, just buffalo grass.

Crossing the Platte River was tricky when its waters rose. Some wagons had removable wheels so they could float across the river like rafts.

In the Rockies, a blizzard could halt the wagons. The temperature sometimes dipped to 40° below.

Men, called scouts, who knew the trails, rode ahead. They watched for Indians and picked the easiest path. Horses and oxen were precious to the pioneers. You could lose them to Indians or to an accident on the trail.

It took two long months to cross the Great Plains.

In the summer it was like an oven, hot and dry. The land was full of buffalo, antelope and other animals to hunt. It also had coyotes and wolves who hunted your cows. Rain turned the dust to mud, hard going for wagons. Often it seemed as if they would never reach the end. But, on they rolled.

Indians watched the wagon trains crossing their lands. What did the strangers want?

At sunset, the wagons stopped.

It had been a good day. They had covered almost twenty miles. A

group of Indians came to talk. The leader of the wagon train gave them tobacco and some colored ribbons. Music would be played.

The wagons were formed in a tight circle for protection. Children gathered dried buffalo manure, called chips, for the fires. Women cooked stew and baked cornbread. After supper the pioneers told stories and joked. Some read the bible. Sleep came easily after a day of walking. Guards kept watch. A coyote's howl was heard.

A game of wrestling.

Oregon at last!

There were forests full of deer, grizzly bears and wolverines. Salmon and trout swam in crystal clear streams. With the help of their neighbors, each family quickly built a log cabin before winter came. Wooden planks were used for the roof. The cabin had only one window, covered with a piece of oiled paper or a greased deerskin. The children gathered moss to stuff mattresses. When their shoes and clothing wore out, the pioneers made new ones from deerskin. Sometimes they cut pieces from the old wagon's canvas cover. There was a lot to be done!

Large rocks had to be moved.

Plowing the fields

Husking corn

Washing clothes

Oregon City was one of the first towns to be built. Going there to shop was a real event for the new settlers.

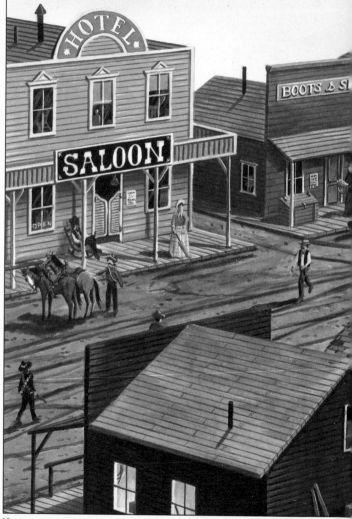

On Sunday, they went to church. Some walked for hours to get there. They met friends and praised God.

The **blacksmith** was an important
person in town. He made shoes
for horses and nails for building.
If your plow was broken, he could
fix it. His hammer rang like
a bell and sparks flew.
At the **saloon** men played cards
and passed on the latest news.
What was happening "back East"
in the states they came from?

Sometimes, all seemed calm at the **sheriff's** office. But he often spent a night in the saddle. Chasing a dangerous outlaw could take him a hundred miles.

At the **general store**, you could find almost anything! Women brought corn, wheat, eggs and vegetables from their farms. They traded for needles and ribbon; pots and pans. They needed sugar and coffee and, maybe, a treat for the children, hard candy.

**Once a year, in the spring,
ranchers hired extra cowboys.**
This was for the "round up."
The cattle and newborn calves
were brought to a central spot.
Red-hot irons were used to put
the ranch's mark on the calves.
Then they formed herds of a
thousand or more, driving them
north to the railroad lines.
Dodge City and Abilene in Kansas
were famous as **cow towns.**

Lassos were not simple ropes. They were
made of sturdy braided leather.

Driving a herd of cattle was hard
work...long hours chasing strays and
pushing the slow ones along. At night
cowboys took turns guarding the herd.
There were many dangers: wolves,
storms, and especially, **rustlers**.
These were gangs of thieves who stole
cattle. At the cow town the cattle were
sold for the best price. Then they were
loaded on trains and sent to the East.

Cowboys wore wide-brimmed hats to protect them from the rain and sun. A bandanna, worn around the neck, could be pulled up to keep dust off their faces. Leather **chaps** over their pants protected them from brambles. Thick gloves and boots were needed. **Cowboys wore these same clothes, day after day!** The horses they rode usually belonged to the ranch. Their guns might be their only possessions.

What is a **rodeo?**
It is a Spanish word which first meant "round-up" before the long spring drive. Later it came to mean a public contest or sport. Cowboys win prize money for the best **bronco** rider and calf-roper.

Riding a bronco in a corral for livestock.

Cowboys marking cattle with the ranch's brand.

Fur trappers were called Mountain Men.

Animal furs were valuable.
Trappers set off to hunt for
many months in the Rockies.
They brought back raccoon,
muskrat and, especially,
beaver pelts (the fur and skin).
Every gentleman in the cities
wanted a beaver hat to wear.

At sundown, a trapper,
dressed in deerskin,
sets a trap by a beaver lodge.

The trapper often befriended Indians,
and sometimes married an Indian
woman.
During the winter, he and his wife
cleaned, stretched, and dried the
skins on the walls of their cabin.
Then he would bring his furs, tied
in bundles, to merchants from large
companies. He traded them for more
traps, gunpowder, bullets and tobacco.
Mountain men were often the first
white men to see places like
Great Salt Lake and Yosemite.

The Indians did not always attack forts...

At the start of the westward movement, these large buildings were used as trading posts. An Indian could trade beaver pelts and buffalo hides. He got steel knives, iron pots, mirrors and other useful goods.

But more and more white men
entered the Indians' hunting
grounds. They killed too many
buffalo and took too much land.
The Indians felt robbed.
They attacked settlers' homes.
Bitter wars began. To protect
the settlers, the United States
Army bought the forts. Cavalry
and foot soldiers were sent to
man the forts. The Indians lost
the wars and much of their lands.

Prospectors wash pans of sand to
sift out flakes or nuggets of gold.

Gold in California and the Rockies!

In 1848 gold and silver ore was
discovered in California, at a
place called Sutter's Mill. Many
cowboys and settlers left their
jobs to become **prospectors**. Men
from all over the world joined
the gold rush. All it took was a
shovel and pick, a pan and luck.

Mining camps and boom towns
sprung up wherever gold was
found. But after the gold
was gone, they often became
ghost towns.

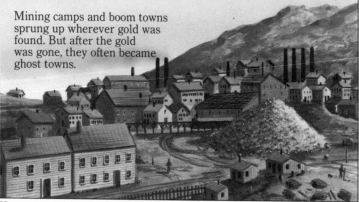

A prospector worked a **claim,** a piece of land on which only he could dig. A law protected his rights from "claim jumpers." By panning in a stream, or using a special box, he washed out the soft earth, leaving heavier gold. A rich claim was called a **strike**. A prospector might work with two or three companions. They had a hard life, away from wives and children. Their dream was to "strike it rich." Then they could go home like kings.

Sometimes they had to dig deep in a mountain to follow the gold trail. Many men died when a mine caved in.

Freight companies were started
once the West was well-populated.
Teams of horses pulled the stage-
coaches of Wells, Fargo. They
carried mail, packages and
passengers. At night they stopped
at stations to sleep and eat.
From Missouri to California it
was an uncomfortable 25-day trip.

But it had taken the pioneers
up to six months to travel the
same distance!
In 1860 the **Pony Express** began.
Young men, riding fast horses,

Sometimes a train was stopped by
outlaws. When buffalo got on
the tracks, the "cow-catcher"
was used to push them off.

carried pouches of mail. Jumping
from one horse to the next, they
rode up to 75 miles without stop.
The charge for a letter was ten
dollars in gold!
This famous service was ended
with the building of **telegraph
lines** across the land. A message
could be sent by electric wires.
In 1869 another great work was
completed, a railroad to the West.

Buffalo Bill

His real name was William F. Cody. He got his nickname as a top hunter of buffalo (meat for the railroad workers). As a young man he was a Pony Express rider and scout. Later he owned a Wild West show which toured the world.

James Butler Hickok

"Wild Bill" Hickok, a famous army scout, stage driver and lawman. He ruled tough towns like Abilene and Hays City with an iron hand. An expert shot, Wild Bill killed many outlaws. He was shot in the back and died in the Dakotas.

Do you know the story of Davy Crockett? He was one of the first pioneers. We still hear about his bear hunting and his coonskin cap. He died in a famous battle at the Alamo in Texas. Like Davy, many people wanted to see what was "over the next hill." The West was tamed and settled by men and women like that.

Martha Canary, known as Calamity Jane, often dressed like a man. She did men's jobs, like Indian scout and freight wagon driver. And she could use that rifle she carried! Calamity was in Hays City in the same years as Wild Bill Hickok. One story is that they were sweethearts.

Calamity Jane

Oh My Darling
Clementine

1. In a ca- vern, in a ca- nyon, Ex- ca-
Refrain Oh my dar- ling, oh my dar- ling, oh my

-va- ting for a mine Dwelt a mi- ner, for- ty-
dar- ling Cle- men- tine! Thou art lost and for- go-

-ni- ner, And his daugh- ter Cle- men- tine.
for ever, Dread — ful sorry Cle- men- tine.

In a cavern, in a canyon,
Excavating for a mine
Lived a miner, forty-niner
and his daughter Clementine.

Refrain: Oh, my darling, oh, my darling,
Oh, my darling Clementine
You are lost and gone forever
Dreadful sorry, Clementine

Light she wasn't, like a fairy
And her shoes were number nine
Herring boxes, without soxes
Sandals were for Clementine.

Index

Books of Discovery for children five through ten...

Young Discovery Library is an international undertaking — the series is now published in nine countries. It is the world's first pocket encyclopedia for children, 120 titles will be published.

Each title in the series is an education on the subject covered: a collaboration among the author, the illustrator, an advisory group of elementary school teachers and an academic specialist on the subject.

The goal is to respond to the endless curiosity of children, to fascinate and educate.

TITLES IN THIS SERIES:

The Barbarians

Odile Bombarde

Here's a complete introduction to the tribes that came to conquer and stayed to settle Europe in the Middle Ages—featuring pictures and descriptions of Attila, the Vikings, Charlemagne and more.

Crocodiles and Alligators

Marie Farré

The daily lives, evolution, eggs, babies and other natural history of the big reptiles from the time they were worshiped in ancient Egypt to today—plus a poem by Lewis Carroll.

Monkeys, Apes and Other Primates

André Lucas

Entertainment and education both abound—as these realistic renderings show dozens of species and engaging text tells why lemurs stay up all night, gorillas are strong, gibbons fly—and more!

Going West: Cowboys and Pioneers

Martine Courtault

Adventures of the pioneers, including details of a two-month trip across the Great Plains, life during the Gold Rush, settling a new town, the Pony Express and everyday life in the old west.

Bears, Big and Little

Pierre Pferrer

Are bears as clumsy as they seem, what do grizzlies eat, how do mother bears raise their young? This book answers these and other important questions as it describes all eight species of bears and their habitats.

Long Ago in a Castle

Marie Farré

Realistic rendering of many castles across Europe open this book-full of facts about castle communities of the Middle Ages—replete with information on building techniques, home life, knights, feasts and lords.

Following Indian Trails

Nicholas Grenier

Information to defy stereotypes and teach how Native Americans came to this land, acquired horses, built villages, taught children about life and protected their land.

Undersea Giants

Patrick Geistdoerfer

Poetry, lore, authoritative renderings and text join in this introduction to whales, seals, dolphins and other sea mammals—with many fascinating facts about communication, reproduction and protection of the species.